Walking and Strolling

By Cameron Macintosh

A long walk is good for us!

It can be fun.

And it can help with stress.

You do not have to sprint.
Just go for a quick stroll!

If you stroll in spring,
you will spot lots of plants.

Some plants have
strong smells.
Pick a big bunch
and bring it home!

Bring a pack
on a long stroll.

Slip on the straps,
and off you go!

Sit on this bench
and have a rest.
Munch on lunch!

Then stroll up this big hill!

You can spot a finch
on the branch of a shrub.

A long stroll can be such a big thrill!

I have a hunch that you will love it.

CHECKING FOR MEANING

1. What will you see on a stroll in spring? *(Literal)*
2. Where might you see a finch? *(Literal)*
3. Why should you bring a backpack on a long stroll? *(Inferential)*

EXTENDING VOCABULARY

stroll	What is a stroll? If you go for a stroll, do you walk quickly or slowly?
munch	How many sounds are in the word *munch*? What is another word the author could have used instead of *munch*?
shrub	Which consonant blend is in the word *shrub*? What is another word the author could have used instead of *shrub*?

MOVING BEYOND THE TEXT

1. Why is going for a walk good for stress? Do you ever feel stressed? What do you do to feel better?
2. What are some reasons people might like to go for a walk in spring? Which other seasons might be a good time to go for a walk? Why?
3. What animals and birds might you see on a walk around your neighbourhood?
4. Have you ever been on a long walk or a hike? Why is it important to rest sometimes on a long walk?

SPEED SOUNDS

PRACTICE WORDS

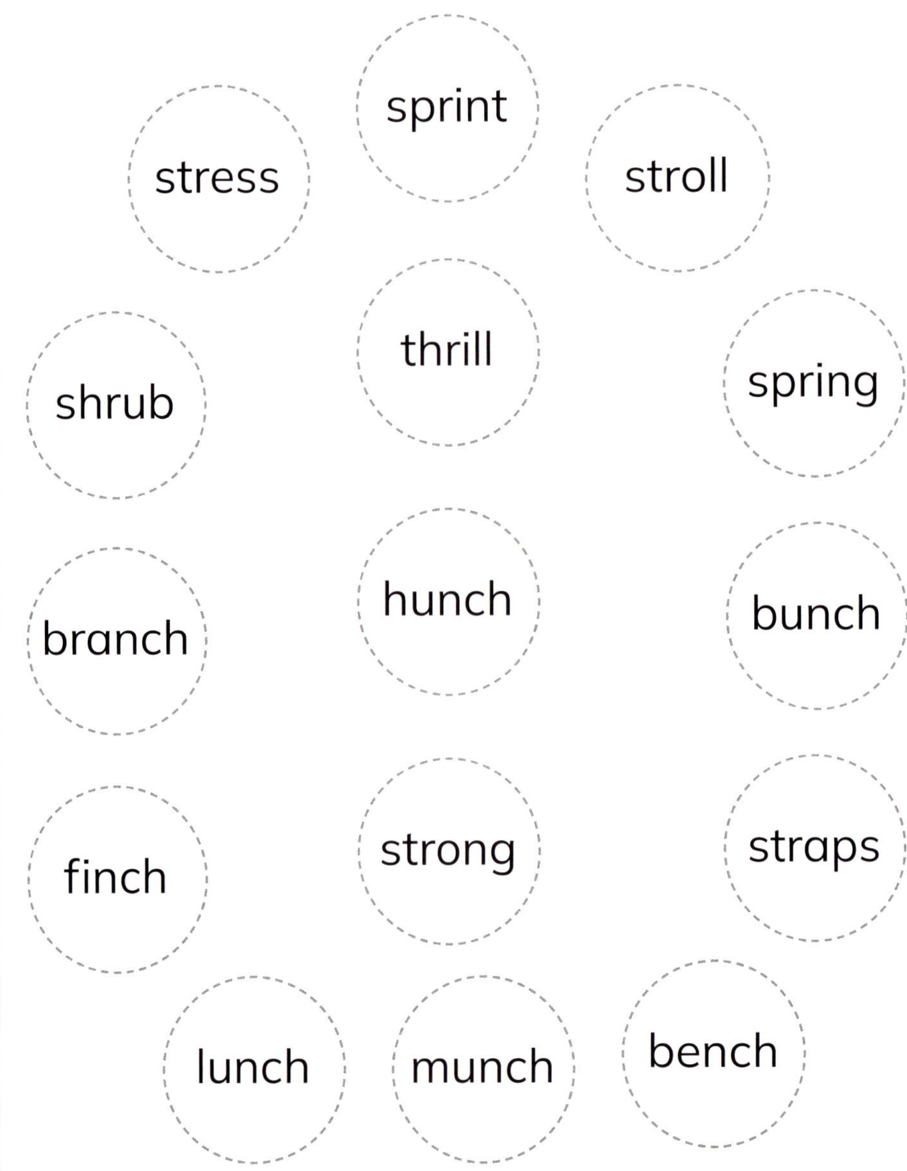